ANG[...] POWER

'Once upon a time there were three very different little girls ... who grew up to be three very different women. They have three things in common. They're brilliant. They're beautiful. And they work for me.

My name is Charlie ...'

CHARLIE'S ANGELS™

PENGUIN BOOKS

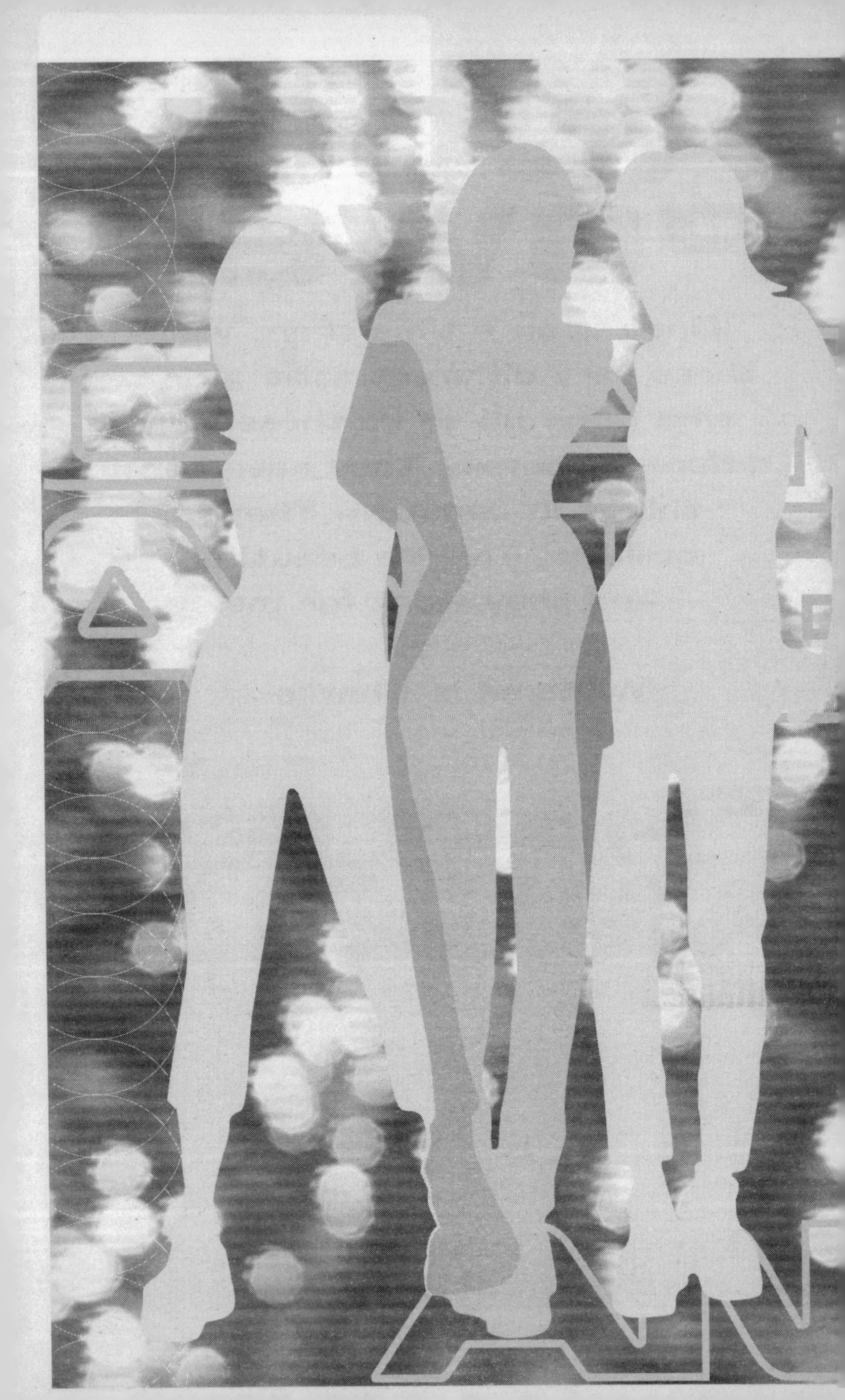

angel power

ACTION FILE

PENGUIN BOOKS

Published by the Penguin Group
Penguin Books Ltd, 27 Wrights Lane, London W8 5TZ, England
Penguin Putnam Inc., 375 Hudson Street, New York, New York 10014, USA
Penguin Books Australia Ltd, Ringwood, Victoria, Australia
Penguin Books Canada Ltd, 10 Alcorn Avenue, Toronto, Ontario, Canada M4V 3B2
Penguin Books India (P) Ltd, 11 Community Centre, Panchsheel Park,
New Delhi – 110 017, India
Penguin Books (NZ) Ltd, Cnr Rosedale and Airborne Roads, Albany, Auckland,
New Zealand
Penguin Books (South Africa) (Pty) Ltd, 5 Watkins Street, Denver Ext 4,
Johannesburg 2094, South Africa

On the World Wide Web at: www.penguin.com

Penguin Books Ltd, Registered Offices: Harmondsworth, Middlesex, England

First published 2000
1 3 5 7 9 10 8 6 4 2

Made and printed in England by Clays Ltd, St Ives plc

British Library Cataloguing in Publication Data
A CIP catalogue record for this book is available from the British Library

ISBN 0–141–31082–0

Samantha Cole is a writer's name for Stephen Cole

CHARLIE'S ANGELS

There's an old saying – Fools rush in where Angels fear to tread. But Charlie's Angels don't know the meaning of fear – and any opponent who comes up against them is the real fool! When the Angels' fists start flying, their foes start flying faster … They're a fearless female fighting force who take on the world's toughest challenges and come out on top: Natalie, Dylan and Alex – Charlie's Angels!

Wherever the action is hottest, that's where you'll find the Angels. When the going gets tough, they don't use guns to fight their way out – just their brilliant minds, natural charms, and some of the neatest gadgets and fighting skills in the world.

Throughout this book, you'll find you have unrestricted access to the Angels' dangerous hip-and-happening world. Discover their secrets, their tricks of the trade, how they relax when they're off duty, and take some Angelic tips on how you can make Angel Power work for *you*!

Contents

angel power

Angel Power

angel

MEET CHARLIE'S

JUST WHO IS

All-seeing, yet always unseen, reclusive millionaire Charlie is the Angels' main man. He brought them together to fight crime and, as head of the Charles Townsend Detective Agency, he gives them only the most top-level assignments. When only the best is good enough, it's Charlie's Angels who deliver every time.

No one knows why Charlie will never reveal his true identity to the Angels, only ever speaking to them from afar. Has he got something to hide? Is he someone they already know? Is he a secret agent whose cover must never be blown? Your guess is as good as the Angels' … and they're always kept too busy to worry for long about who he might be!

As for where Charlie is based, it's hard to tell. When he contacts the Angels he could be

ANGELS ...
CHARLIE, ANYWAY?

anywhere: halfway up a mountain, shark-diving in the Pacific, or even standing a few metres away! And when he isn't risking his life just for the thrill of it, Charlie retreats to his hideout – a small but tastefully furnished cabin on a gorgeous beach in some American beauty spot, a simple place to escape the pressures of his top-level world. But with a new case for Charlie's Angels never far away, it's a sure bet he's not there for long. Whatever else may be going on in his secret life, Charlie cares deeply for all the Angels. He keeps the jobs coming and looks after his team in sophisticated style.

angel file 1

ALEXANDRA 'ALEX' MUNDAY

ALEX

Born: 5 December 1975

Hair: Long, dark

Eyes: Dark brown

Height: 5'3"

Marital status: Single (but totally into movie actor boyfriend Jason Gibbons)

Background: Coming from a wealthy, successful family – her parents were professors at Harvard University – Alex consistently outclassed her fellow

pupils in all subjects at boarding school, excelling in particular at horse riding and athletics. Completing her studies when just thirteen years old, Alex spent her teenage years having adventures all over the world: studying and training under a Tibetan guru, working on top-secret assignments with a double agent in Paris, dancing with the Stuttgart Ballet ... After a spell working for NASA as an engineer and electronics consultant, Alex found she craved adventure too much just to sit in an office – and so became one of Charlie's Angels!

Special skills: Computer hacking, fencing, expert in martial arts

Description: A sultry, sophisticated, feminine powerhouse, Alex is a class act. Her excellent all-round education has left her supremely confident and able to turn her hand to anything from defusing a bomb to playing electric guitar. The only thing she can't do is cook – her blueberry muffins are more like blueberry rock cakes!

angel

Born: 23 May 1976

Hair: Medium length, auburn

Eyes: Green

***Height*:** 5'5"

***Marital status*:** Single

Background: Dylan's mother died when she was a child and she never met her father. She grew up in a rough neighbourhood, where she soon learnt she had to play tough in order to survive. Graduating with only average grades, Dylan joined a police academy, but was asked to leave when she punched out the bullying instructor! After spending some years travelling America, working in dead-end jobs but learning some valuable life lessons, Dylan found she'd picked up more than enough essential skills to become an ace Angel for Charlie.

Special skills: Hand-to-hand combat, skydiving, covert entry

Description: Dylan is full of attitude, impetuous with an explosive temper and a fierce fighting style. But hiding behind the rough and tumble front is a sensitive girl – while she loves the glamour of international crime-fighting, she hates injustice of any kind. Her determination to win through against the toughest odds and save the day is truly incredible.

angel file 3

NATALIE COOK

***Born*:** 13 July 1977

Hair: Platinum blonde

Eyes: Pale blue

Height: 5'9"

Marital status: Single

Background: Always the slightly geeky one at school – tall and gangly with glasses, braces and endless bad-hair days – Natalie used her head and excelled at all subjects, especially science. Her brains came in very handy for winning dozens of TV game shows' cash prizes when putting herself through university to get her PhD. While studying, she also found time to pass her advanced driving test in record time and developed a passion for any form of transport. After a spell as a Research Scientist at the Swedish National Academy and a US Navy test pilot, Natalie found herself wanting to use her skills in a more proactive way – and so became one of Charlie's Angels.

Special skills: Driving, gadgets, general knowledge

Description: Although Natalie has grown up into a beautiful and sophisticated woman, she still remembers her slightly nerdy schooldays and worries that she doesn't always fit in. Fearless and loyal, with a quicksilver mind, Natalie keeps her head – and all those around her safe – no matter what.

special angel file

JOHN BOSLEY

Background: Bosley has known Charlie for longer than any of the Angels, and is the only person Charlie contacts directly – so, for security reasons, his background is classified.

Additional info: In fact, Bosley has come closer than anyone to actually seeing Charlie in the flesh. When dropping off documents to the great man's beach cabin, Bosley saw a hand reach out from behind the door to pick them up ... It's not much of a sighting, but it's more than anyone else can boast!

Special skills: Bosley's sense of humour lightens even the tensest moments – and his honest advice works for the Angels every time. He's also prepared to take on anything at a moment's notice, no matter how crazy or dangerous – from eating potentially fatal pufferfish sushi to taking over the steering of a car in the middle of a frantic chase.

Description: Bosley's enthusiasm for undercover work means he sometimes gets carried away and a little out of his depth – and the Angels have to come to the rescue! He admires and adores Dylan, Natalie and Alex in equal measure, and would do – and frequently does – anything for them. Their safety is his number-one concern – as is Bosley's to the Angels. Together, they make an unbeatable team!

TOP-SECRET CASEFILE

THE ERIC KNOX AFFAIR

CHARLIE'S MISSION BRIEFING

Perhaps you've heard of Eric Knox – a brilliant engineer and founder of a new software company (Knox Technologies) specializing in communications. Young, handsome and soon to be a multi-millionaire, Knox was kidnapped last night at a charity ball. No ransom has been demanded, no message from the kidnappers given. Knox has vanished, Angels, and it's your job to find out where he's gone and to get him back!

As for the motive ... well, Knox has created a computer program of phenomenal power. It can take a recording of a person's voice and process it digitally, so that a central computer can hold a match on file. You could say he's decoded pure audio DNA! Using spy satellites in orbit, the technology can be used to trace any person talking on a phone – even me! – to absolutely anywhere in the world. If the software falls into the wrong hands it's the end of privacy, the end of security – and way too much power for any one shadowy schemer to have.

THE PLAYERS

We've talked about Knox – now let's see who else is starring in this high-tech, high-octane drama ...

VIVIAN WOOD

Partner and co-chairman of Eric Knox's company, the cool and beautiful Vivian Wood is also one of his closest friends. She's hired you, Angels, to locate Knox and get him back no matter what. Although there's been no word from the kidnappers, she's convinced he's alive.

As a person she's not the most likeable client: she's difficult, a little arrogant, aloof – and she's impatient for results. Don't let her rush you, Angels. I think there's more to her than meets the eye ... even at this distance! Keep on your guard!

ROGER CORWIN

Owner of Red Star International, Knox Technologies' biggest rival, Corwin is a mean-looking man; a man who would sell his own mother if it advanced his business. A jet-setting playboy, Corwin's a crude and obvious man, but his power and riches make him very, very dangerous.

He has a lot to gain from Knox going down. Possessing that voice-mapping technology – together with his incredible hold over the world's communications satellites – would open a billion doors into blackmail, corruption and exploitation. If he's guilty, Angels – bring him down!

THE THIN MAN

We don't have much information on this individual, but he's been glimpsed at trouble spots the world over, and most recently at any function where you'll find Roger Corwin or Eric Knox. He's a very nasty fighter, an expert in unarmed combat, gymnastics and any device of death you could care to mention. He's utterly ruthless and sets out to win at any cost, no matter what the danger. It's like a game to him. But when you go up against him, Angels, you're playing for your lives.

And even if you find Eric Knox alive, I have a feeling that that could be just the start of our problems ...

MESSAGE ENDS

WHICH ANGEL ARE YOU?

Each of Charlie's Angels is very different – but even if they sometimes disagree about the way to do something, they always get the job done!

Think you're ready to take the Angel Challenge? Read the quiz questions below and make a note of the answers that most closely describe what *you'd* do. When you're through, check the results and see which Angel you're closest to!

1. It's Sunday night, and your last chance to chill before spending another week foiling endless bad guys. Do you ...?

a) call up some friends, snuggle down with a video and get an early night.

b) make some muffins to take in for your friends the next day.

c) get some mates together for one last, quick end-of-weekend party.

2. You're trying to impress a guy you like. Do you ...?

a) tell him he's gorgeous – in a foreign language.

b) strike a gravity-defying yoga pose until his eyes are out on stalks.

c) fix his TV set that's been on the blink for weeks in thirty seconds.

3. You're giving chase to a bad guy who's just made it to his car. Do you ...?

a) slide under the car and fix it so it's going nowhere.

b) slug him one through the car window.

c) leap into another car and prepare to give chase.

4. A villain tells you he's hidden a bomb in a busy restaurant. Do you ...?

a) swiftly and efficiently evacuate all the diners.

b) swiftly pinpoint the bomb with an etheric beam locator and disarm it.

c) force the bad guy to reveal the bomb then sling it out into the river where it can go off out of harm's way.

5. You're going undercover in a finishing school for girls. Do you pose as ...?

a) a bored wild child who wishes she was somewhere else.

b) a royal princess, already perfectly groomed.

c) a quiet, well-behaved girl who's happy to learn.

6. In an ideal world, would you chase after bad guys ...?

a) in a red Ferrari.

b) in the first thing that came to hand.

c) on horseback.

7. Bosley is feeling down in the dumps. Do you ...?

a) take him out with some of your friends for a party.

b) offer to play him at Trivial Pursuits.

c) offer to cook him something nice.

8. Your date asks you what you'd like to do tonight. Do you say you want to ...?

a) go to a sophisticated restaurant for dinner.

b) just chill out and kick back in your favourite cafe.

c) go dancing at a hot night-spot in town.

9. You and your fellow Angels must rescue a kidnap victim from a boat bristling with villains. Would you rather ...?

a) put on your wetsuit, sneak aboard and disable the boat's radar systems.

b) parachute into the action, land on the boat and high-kick your way through the bad guys.

c) steer your own ship alongside the kidnappers' so the others can leap aboard and escape with the victim.

10. The weekend is here again. Are you planning ...?

a) a little dancing, a little studying and a lot of sleep.

b) a little horse riding, a little baking and a lot of relaxation.

c) a lot of fun, a lot of action and a little sleep.

WHO ARE YOU?

Match your answers against the ones below to find out which Angel is closest to YOU.

1 a) Natalie b) Alex c) Dylan
2 a) Natalie b) Dylan c) Alex
3 a) Alex b) Dylan c) Natalie
4 a) Natalie b) Alex c) Dylan
5 a) Dylan b) Alex c) Natalie
6 a) Natalie b) Dylan c) Alex
7 a) Dylan b) Natalie c) Alex
8 a) Alex b) Dylan c) Natalie
9 a) Alex b) Dylan c) Natalie
10 a) Natalie b) Alex c) Dylan

MOSTLY ALEX

You're a class act who is cool, sophisticated and totally in control – but with a warm heart and a caring, sharing attitude to life. A whizz with gadgets and all things technical, you also love elegance and the finer things in life – as well as being an active Angel at all times!

MOSTLY DYLAN

You've got quite an attitude on you! You play hard and work hard. In a tough situation you'll take the quickest route out – even if it's the hardest. You have the guts and determination to see anything through, and you don't like to feel a minute of your life is being wasted!

MOSTLY NATALIE

You're super-cool, but you're so busy looking out for others you barely realize it. You don't need to cause a scene to be the centre of attention. Intelligent and sensitive, you're level-headed and will always look before you leap. You're dependable and you'd never let a friend down.

WINNING COMBINATION

How did you do? Did your answers match one Angel every time or did you come out a combination of all three? It doesn't really matter either way, because each of the Angels is one of life's winners – and if you're like them at all, you're bursting with Angel Power too!

Good-to-go GADGETS

When Charlie's Angels leap into action they're often on their own – undercover and under threat from a whole host of hoods, henchmen and all-round bad guys. They need the very best protection they can get to do their job – to infiltrate enemy headquarters, gather surveillance information and, most importantly, to stay alive! Which is why Charlie spares no expense to make sure his girls have the very latest in high-cost crime-busting, super spy technology.

Now you can check out the incredible high-tech world of the Angels, and the gizmos that help them wade through even the toughest assignments like they're taking a Sunday stroll in the park ...

MOLAR MICROPHONE

This tiny wireless mic squeezes into place over the top of one of your back teeth, and transmits crystal-clear sound to anyone with a receiver tuned to its secret frequency. It may not taste fantastic, but it's essential for those more dangerous missions – just don't end up swallowing the thing! When the Angels and Bosley go undercover at Roger Corwin's swanky high-society party to learn the whereabouts of Eric Knox, they each use a molar mic to help them stay in touch. Little does

Bosley know that all their lives – and also Charlie's – may depend on his molar mic ...

FINGERPRINT SCANNER

In a company like Red Star International it's not enough to have a simple secret password on your PC to keep out prying eyes – especially when those eyes are wide and beautiful and belong to Charlie's Angels! So, working on the principle that fingerprints can't be lost, borrowed or forgotten in the way passwords can, Corwin has had special fingerprint scanners installed – and if your prints don't match, you can't come in!

When the Angels have to infiltrate Red Star International, they get round this tricky security system with typical skill. While Natalie and Alex distract one of Red Star's directors in a bar, Dylan swipes his beer bottle and takes it back to base to scan the fingerprints into their own computer. Cloning the fingerprint and outputting it to a thin rubbery film, they can then stick it on their own fingers to fool the computer systems – helping them get into the very heart of Red Star International to find out just what Corwin is really up to ...

RETINAL SCANNER

Even if you manage to foil Corwin's fingerprint security precautions, your problems aren't over. He's also installed special retinal scanners: machines that identify a person by scanning their eyeballs. No matter how much you flutter your lashes, if your retina's not recognized, the alarms will be blaring in the blink of a mismatched eye.

The Angels take an unusual approach to getting hold of a Red Star director's eye-print. Dressed as Bavarian dancers, they hide a retinal scanner in a tuba and call round at the director's home to sneakily steal the ideal eye image. Back at base, they print it onto a contact lens that, when worn, will disguise the wearer's real retina. It *should* be enough to fool the security systems into letting the Angels in ...

VOICE-SYNTHESIZER CHIP

The voice-synthesizer chip is a very handy gadget that changes the way your voice sounds – you can even sound like someone of the opposite sex! So, you can fool your enemies over the phone or, if you're also wearing a cool disguise, you can become a completely new person. Even your best mate wouldn't recognize you! The chip works by scanning the sound waves formed by your voice box and converting them into tones that are higher or lower, depending on who you want to sound like. When turning on the charm isn't enough to save the Angels in a tricky situation, they simply turn on the voice chip and talk their way out of trouble!

NIGHT-VISION COSMETICS

The Angels must often work at night, in the dark, out of sight – which can be dangerous if they need to signal to Bosley that they require back-up! So Charlie has provided them with a very special kind of make-up. In natural light, the eyeshadow and lipstick look just like the Angels' typically sophisticated, expensive cosmetics. But when viewed through special ultraviolet contact lenses, they sparkle like stardust – so even in pitch blackness an Angel can light up the night!

REVERSE-VISION SUNGLASSES

In a combat situation, the Angels never know where the next attack will come from. They really do need eyes in the back of their heads – which is why they sometimes use special spy sunglasses that let you look behind while staring straight ahead! Available on the Internet now, the special mirrored lenses show who's following you every time you look to one side – something Alex could've used when she came up against the Thin Man!

FIBRE-OPTICS SCOPE

This is an essential device for secret surveillance, allowing the Angels to spy on their suspects wherever they're hiding! The optical cable is thinner than a wire and flexible too, so it can slide under doors, through cracks and round corners with no problem. Once it's in place, you just look into the collapsible eyepiece to see what's going down! Sadly, the Angels have never been close enough to Charlie to slide one round a corner or under a door to find out just what their boss really looks like ...

SOUND-LOOP GENERATOR

When the Angels are being briefed by Charlie, extra security precautions are taken just in case anyone's thinking of listening in. Tiny amplifiers are hidden throughout the office, which generate noise on frequencies that humans can't hear and which any hidden microphones can't deal with. So when the eavesdropper tries to listen in to his hidden bugs, all he'll hear is a noise like a loud car alarm!

CONCEALED CAMERAS

When a more subtle sort of spying is called for, the Angels have no end of high-tech, miniature video cameras specially designed to fit into ordinary objects like a briefcase handle, a brooch or even a mobile phone! Fitting these cameras into place often proves dangerous, but the information they provide can be essential. The camera relays its pictures to a special receiver attached to a monitor – so Bosley can keep an eye on what's going on from the comfort of his armchair back in the office!

STAYING AHEAD

There are dozens of other mind-boggling gadgets that Dylan, Natalie and Alex use every day – from invisible-ink pens to digital transmitters, from coin-sized cameras to night-vision contacts. And Charlie makes sure their gear is the hottest you can get. Because with the bad guys getting worse and the fighting getting dirtier, staying one step ahead is crucial – and that means confounding the enemy with every high-tech trick in the virtual book!

M.E.N.ACES

Charlie's Angels operate in a tough, dangerous criminal underworld – but with their experience, looks, intelligence and charm, they're more than a match for any of the guys they come up against. Macho men just can't compete with the smouldering mix of feminine intuition and graceful action moves.

In everyday life too, a girl has to stick up for herself in all sorts of ways. In this chapter, let Charlie's Angels show you how you can put yourself first and get in touch with your own unique Angel Power!

THE BAD OLD DAYS

Have you ever caught old comedy shows on TV? The kind where a man comes through the door and yells 'Hi, honey, I'm home!' His wife greets him with a kiss and asks about his day at the office while she's been left in the house tidying or cooking dinner …

What's so funny about these shows today is the idea that a woman could have nothing better to do than wait around for her man to come back from work so she could look after him!

Luckily things have changed. Both at home and in the workplace, women have as important a role to play as any man. And, of course, there are some ultra-cool jobs that women are uniquely qualified for – like being an Angel-for-hire at the Charles Townsend Detective Agency!

EVERY ANGEL'S GUIDE TO DATING

While being a stylish, top-secret private investigator brings endless glamour and excitement, it also brings more than its fair share of problems and hassles – the biggest being trying to hold down a relationship when your life's in danger on a high-level confidential assignment every day!

And despite being blessed with brains and beauty, the Angels still find dating the trickiest business of all. When it comes to captivating guys, they each go about it in very different ways! Here is some boy advice straight from the Angels' mouths. Will their tips work for you?

1. SETTING YOUR SIGHTS

So, you've seen this really cool guy around ... but he doesn't know you're alive?

ALEX: How do you know? Chances are he noticed you long ago! These days there's no need to wait for the guy to make the first move. Be bold. Just casually walk up to him and ask him a simple question – something like, 'Hey, could you tell me what time it is?' When he answers, act a little shocked, tell him you're late for something totally awesome ... then smile, turn and walk away. He'll think you're way cool! And who knows, next time he could be coming up to you to ask the questions ...

NATALIE: This is a bad situation ... I'm a bit too shy to go striding up to him without a warm-up. I'd make a note of who his friends are, see if any of them hang around with people I know. Make a few inquiries as to whether he's as cute on the inside as he is on the outside – and to find out if he's single! If I was still interested, then maybe I'd leave a little note in his locker – something light-hearted, jokey, nothing too serious to freak him out! If I was feeling really brave, I'd even sign it ...

DYLAN: I'd *make* him know I was alive! I'd join the same clubs or sports teams as him, whip up a bit of a storm in the area ... That way I'd be getting more from life myself and I'd keep showing up in his life too! Then, once he realized just how outgoing I was, I'd probably smile at him, maybe chat a little ... make him see what fun we could have together and then walk away! That would turn things around – he'd soon be wondering if I knew that *he* was alive!

2. THE NEXT STEP

So you've met a nice guy and you want to get to know him a bit better ... what are you going to do?

ALEX: If you know you like him, just ask him what he's doing after his classes ... Would he like someone gorgeous to walk him home? Would he like to come with you to support your fave sports team? Make it clear you think it would be cool to spend a little time with him.

NATALIE: If I was into him, I'd probably ask him to do something casual at first, see if he wanted to come for a bike ride with me or go for a run or something ... That way, I wouldn't have to spend the whole time worrying about what I was going to say next – we'd be too out of breath from all that fast-pedalling, swift-jogging exercise!

DYLAN: I'd be happy spending time with him *and* his friends, get to know the whole gang before focusing in on him. What's the rush? Hanging out together in a crowd will help you see if he's really a nice guy or if he's a bit of a show-off when his friends are around. You want someone who will treat you well and with respect whatever the situation.

3. THE BIG DATE

So you've landed an evening with the guy of your dreams – and suddenly your stomach is filled with butterflies. What will you wear? What will you talk about? How can you make sure the date goes well?

ALEX: First of all, chill out – it's just a date. Being hyper the whole way through isn't going to impress! An hour or two before you meet up, put on your favourite music and just relax. Be confident. Have faith in yourself – he wouldn't be meeting you at all if he didn't think you were worth it.

NATALIE: What's he into? Why not do a bit of research?

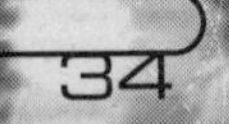

That way, if he wants to talk about the things he loves, you'll be able to join in too and he'll be well impressed! But remember, a good date will want to know all about you too – don't be a walkover and keep the subject on him, him, him all night!

DYLAN: Be yourself – that's the key thing to remember. Dressing yourself up like someone else will only leave you feeling uncomfortable, and you shouldn't have to change yourself to impress a guy! So go along, be laid-back and smile a lot. Don't worry about whether you have a big rosy future together, just enjoy the moment.

MORE MR NICE GUY!

As the Angels have found, there are good men around who treat women equally and with respect! So never settle for second best – and if you're not being treated right, turf that geek right out of your life! Because remember – you've got Angel Power!

AVENGING ANGELS ... FIT TO FIGHT!

The Angels often come up against male opponents in a combat situation, but this can work to their advantage. Macho males think they have little to fear from three pretty women who are *clearly* out of their depth. They think the outcome of the fight's a foregone conclusion. And it is – but in the Angels' favour! Thirty seconds of furious fist-fighting later, those hoods are flat on their backs seeing stars, with only their bruises to hide their blushes!

Dylan, Natalie and Alex have mastered many of the martial arts – they use them in self-defence when fighting crime and also to keep fit both physically and mentally. If you want to boost your own Angel Power you could learn a martial art yourself. But remember – there's much more to these ancient fighting skills than just high-kicking, however easy the Angels make it seem!

Here are three key principles you'd do well to remember if you want to chop, thrust and high-kick with the best of them. Think of them as the three Cs ...

CALM

Even in the heat of the action, you must stay calm and not become flustered. One slip and you could make a big mistake, giving your opponent the upper hand.

COOL

Staying cool and confident under pressure will help you study your enemy, anticipate their moves – and be ready to strike the moment they make a mistake.

CONCENTRATION

Martial arts may seem to be a blur of physical movement – but there's even more going on up top. Concentration – focussing on the fight to the exclusion of all else – is absolutely vital.

FIGHTING STYLES

There are many different kinds of martial art. Some are used exclusively for self-defence. Others are more competitive. All these fighting styles originate from the Far East, and many of them are hundreds of years old.

Budo is the ancient word for the Japanese martial arts. The 'do' part of the word means a path or way to self-improvement through training in those arts, which is why there's a 'do' in Tae Kwon-Do, Aikido and Kendo.

AIKIDO

Aikido translates from the Japanese as 'The way of harmony of the spirit' and, as you might expect from that name, it's one of the more spiritual of the martial arts. That said, it's also incredibly powerful when used in a fighting situation!

When practised as a sport, Aikido is not competitive. Each person proceeds at their own pace and in most Aikido associations there are no opponents, only partners.

There are four important concepts to get to grips with – quite literally! – in Aikido.

Ki

The practising of Aikido is key to developing your 'ki' – a mysterious sense of spirit that will see you through your struggles not just on the throwing mat but in daily life too!

Irimi

Irimi, or 'entering', is exploring the way of moving *into* your partner's attack instead of trying to block it or running away. In this way you can lessen the effectiveness of the attack and put yourself in control.

Ukemi

This is the word for receiving an Aikido throw or 'move'. It refers to the way you roll or break your fall.

Atemi

This is the word given to striking the body, with either the fist or any other weapon. Alex's practising of Atemi leaves her with no fear when facing even the most heavily armed opponents.

Partners take it in turns both to throw and to be thrown, to hit and to be hit. Seeing both sides of the experience is key to your ki's development!

TAE KWON-DO

This form of unarmed combat was developed and perfected in Korea. The words translate as 'The way of smashing with foot and hand' – and when the Angels translate the words into *action*, they show just how devastating this martial art can be!

But, as with all these fighting techniques, Tae Kwon-Do is chiefly concerned with giving its students the confidence to express themselves in their own way. It's not just the best students who are the winners – everyone who learns a new skill or move is considered successful.

There are six belts you can aim to gain in Tae Kwon-Do. Guess which one the Angels own ...

White is the colour of the innocent beginner, a student with no knowledge of the art.

Yellow represents the earth, from which a plant sprouts and takes root, just as the pupil is starting to do as she gets grounded in Tae Kwon-Do.

Green stands for the growth of that plant, as the student's skills develop.

Blue means the heaven towards which the plant is growing, getting stronger all the time – just like the student.

Red signals danger – it reminds the student to be careful and never to lose control of her growing powers.

Black is the opposite of white, signalling how far the student has come from her beginnings – as well as indicating that she is not bothered by either darkness or fear, and is a true Angel!

angel

Bosley, however, hasn't quite got the point of this breathtakingly graceful martial art. If anyone mentions 'Tae Kwon-Do', he makes out they've sneezed and says, 'Bless you!'

KENDO

Kendo means 'The way of the sword' and dates back to around the fifteenth century. It is the art of Japanese Samurai sword fighting. People today don't fight with real swords – they use flexible wooden sticks called *shinai*, and each opponent wears special armour for protection.

During each fight, speed and accuracy of the 'cuts' made by the pretend sword, combined with strong body moves and fierce yells (known as *kiai*), are vital for success. It's a bit like fencing, but players are allowed to use both the edge and the point of the sword to hit targets on their

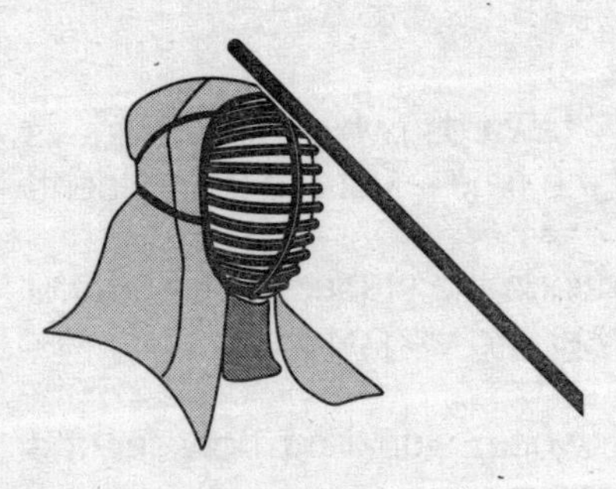

***Men** – A cut to the crown of the head or either of the temples*

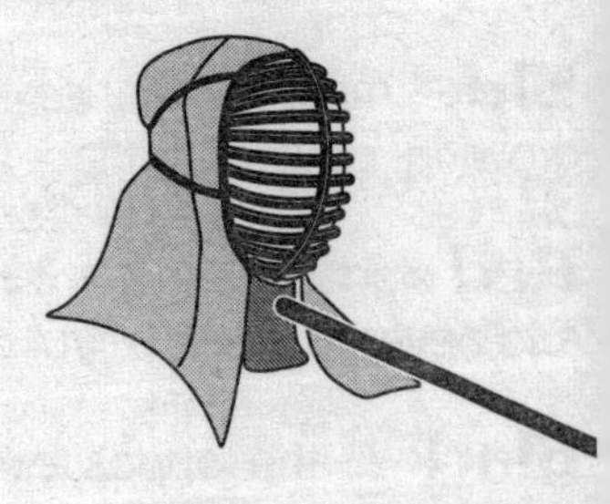

***Tsuki** – A thrust with the tip of the* shinai *to the throat*

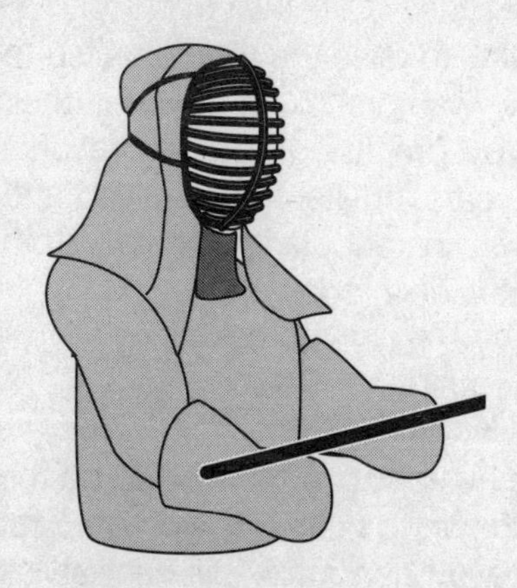

Kote – *A cut to the wrist*

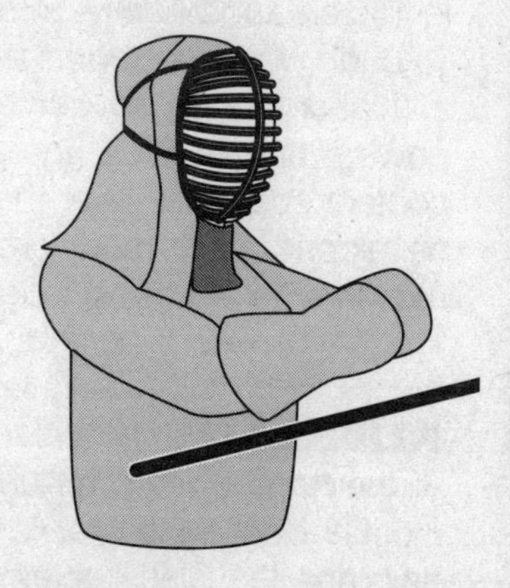

Do – *A cut to either side of the trunk of the body*

opponent's armour. The four main targets are the top of the head, the throat, the stomach area and the wrist.

A contestant wins a match if he or she scores two points, or if only one point has been scored at the end of the fight.

Bosley loves to watch. 'Never say "No can do",' he says. '*Know Kendo* instead!'

JUDO AND JU-JITSU

Judo, meaning 'the gentle way', is a popular martial art. But before Judo there was a more ancient form of this fighting style called Ju-jitsu, which means, 'The practice of the gentle way'. This was the way of fighting practised by the noble Japanese Samurai warriors hundreds of years ago – but when the sword-swinging Samurai began to be replaced by men with guns, the art suffered as the warriors lost heart and became slovenly.

Judo was invented as a way to raise the art of Ju-jitsu to a 'higher plane', to get the warriors excited about their powers and abilities again by practising it as more of a contact sport. But over the years, Ju-jitsu has evolved and developed itself and grown in popularity again. Both movements are being taught widely today.

KUNG FU

All the Angels practise Kung Fu, which is believed to be the most ancient fighting style known to man – or woman! First developed in China, there have been many different styles of Kung Fu passed down through the ages, but perhaps the most Angelic of them all is the Wing Chung system – which was perfected by women over 250 years ago!

The story goes that a Buddhist nun called Ng Mui, who was already a Grand Master of Kung Fu, developed a new fighting technique that favoured speed and style over physical strength – perfect for women to defend themselves from attack. Ng Mui later met a beautiful fifteen-year-old girl named Yim Wing Chun, who was being forced into marriage by a rough, bullying slob. Ng Mui trained Yim Wing Chun in the ways of her new style of Kung Fu, and soon she mastered its distinctive use of finger jabs, elbow strikes and quick-fire use of the knees and feet. She fought back against the bully – and won. Ng Mui named her style of fighting after her young protégée.

Kung Fu is one of the most famous martial arts and is still very popular as a sport today. Unlike the budo disciplines, the emphasis is on attack more than defence, so Kung Fu competitions tend to be incredibly fast and furious events!

WHICH STYLE SUITS?

The Angels use their knowledge of many martial arts to create a fighting style unique to themselves. They take their skills on to the streets, and turn catching the crooks into a sport of their own!

If you decide to try a martial art for yourself, check out your local sports centre for classes, or look on the Internet. If you don't know which one to go for, why not ask to go along to a class and watch? Whichever you choose, remember the old Oriental proverb that says,

'There are many paths at the foot of the mountain, but those who reach the top see the same moon.'

In other words, whichever route you take and however long it takes you, if you persist, the result will be the same – you will be successful – you'll have unlocked the potential of your Angel Power.

When you reach the top yourself and the moon's shining down on you like a celestial spotlight, give a nod to the Angels who got there before you.

NET KNOW-HOW

When Charlie's Angels are in trouble and they need to know something fast, there's a place they can instantly go to find the answer, no matter where they are – just as long as they have a laptop and a phone line at hand! It's the Internet. Alex in particular couldn't live without it! She's always surfing the Net – either for life-saving information or for news and recipes!

The Net is a phenomenal experience, and it's there for everyone. It couldn't be easier to get on to it – if you don't have Internet access at school, perhaps you have a PC at home that can get you connected. Or, failing that, there are Internet cafes popping up all over the place, which are great places for meeting friends, pooling your Angel Power and going surfing together!

WHERE DID IT COME FROM?

The Internet started life over thirty years ago as a few computers connected together. Scientists used them to send messages back and forth and to share knowledge. More and more computers were added to the network and, as it grew, so did the amount of information it could hold.

When the ever-growing net was made available to the general public, it grew even faster – and now it's a truly international network storing some of the most fun and useful stuff you'll ever see – all just a few clicks of your mouse away!

CYBERSPEAK

It's easy to get very technical when talking about the Internet – and while that's fine if you have an IQ like Natalie's, it can seem as if people are talking another language! Here's a quick and easy guide Dylan put together to catch on to what the others are on about!

HARD DRIVE Your computer's 'brain', where all its information is stored.

LOG ON You 'log on' when you connect to the Internet through your computer's modem.

MODEM A box that plugs into your phone line at one end and your computer at the other. It lets your computer talk down the phone line to another computer with a modem.

WORLD WIDE WEB The sum total of all the web sites in cyberspace – a mass of electronic pages stretching right across the Net.

WEB SITE A themed collection of pages on the World Wide Web, set up by a person or an organization.

CYBERSPACE An abstract 'world' of digital information that you access every time you log on to the Internet.

angel

DOWNLOAD What you do when you want to transfer an image or piece of text from the Internet to your own computer's hard drive.

E-MAIL Electronic mail – like sending a letter from your computer, where your e-mail service provider is the post sorting office and your modem is the mailman!

FLAMING To reply to someone's e-mail letting them know in no uncertain terms that they have upset you.

JAVA A programming language that jazzes up pages on the World Wide Web by allowing neat animations and 3D effects to be included.

LINK Certain keywords (often underlined and in blue) on a web site, or certain key graphics that, when clicked on, take you on to another related page either on the same site or somewhere new. This is how you navigate through the World Wide Web.

NEWSGROUP A club existing on the Internet that allows its members to discuss a particular subject by posting messages over their computers.

To go **ON-LINE** To connect to the Internet – if you're 'on-line', you're up and running.

SEARCH ENGINE A free service you go to when you want to look for something in particular on the Internet. You type in the keywords you're searching for and click on 'Go'. The search engine then sorts through the World Wide Web presenting you with a link to any page that seems relevant to your query.

SERVICE PROVIDER A company that allows you access to the Internet.

WHAT'S OUT THERE?

When you connect to the Internet, your start page or 'home' page – your gateway to cyberspace – will contain some kind of search engine. Simply type in what you're looking for – anything from local self-defence classes to cinema times – and the search engine will find a whole lot of possible web sites you can link to that might be able to help.

When Alex needs to know the difference between baking soda and baking powder, it's there on-line. And when Bosley's life depends on the Angels working out a secret location from just a few scattered facts, it's the resources on the web that help them save the day. An almost impossible amount of incredible information is there at your fingertips for the cost of a local call – but remember, you must always get permission from the person paying the phone bill before you go on-line!

NET RULES

Before you set off exploring, there are a few essential rules you need to follow every time you use the Net.

● Never give out your full name or address to strangers on the Net – keep them top secret.

● If you make friends over the Internet, tell your family about them – and remember, whatever anyone says, it's not cool to go along and meet someone you've chatted to on-line by yourself. Never make secret arrangements!

● Chatting is fun, but never stick around in a chat room if

someone's making you feel uncomfortable or worried. You're in control, so you say what's OK – and what's not!

● Be sensible about what you look for – not everything you'll find in cyberspace is helpful. Tell an adult or your teacher if you find something on the Net that makes you feel uncomfortable.

WHAT'S THE NEWS?

Alex is currently dating movie heart-throb Jason Gibbons – and so sometimes, for fun, she logs on to his fan club's newsgroup, to see how popular he is!

If there's a subject you're crazy about, whether it's a sport, a pop group or a movie star, chances are there are lots of people who feel exactly the same way – and they're discussing the latest developments and gossip in a newsgroup right now!

Newsgroups are different from chat rooms. You're not communicating with one person, but a whole group all at once and anyone can reply whenever they like. Joining is free and no one can stop you having your say. Whatever you write and put up for others to read is called a 'posting'. You can start your own conversations or just chip into other people's.

But don't forget, a newsgroup is still a public place in its own way. There's a certain way to behave when you're out there.

NETIQUETTE

Here are some tips on 'Netiquette' that Alex has picked up!

● Never type posts in capital letters – this is the equivalent of shouting, and you'll seem ignorant and rude. Also,

CHARLIE'S ANGELS™

Alex –
Polished perfection

Natalie –
s Natalie's world ...

Dylan –
A sensitive soul

At the Charles Townsend Agency, the Angels relax

Dylan, Bosley and Alex undercover
Corwin's penthouse pa

e Angels
epare to face
e Thin Man in a
inatown alley

At an L. A.
Speedway

CHARLIE'S ANGELS™

The Ange
and Bosl
in disgui

The Angels vis
Red Star Syste
headquarters i
disguise

e agency is destroyed – can the
gels solve the case alone?

CHARLIE'S ANGELS

Eric Knox and Vivian Wood plot to get rid of the Angels

CHARLIE'S ANGELS

Natalie prepares to fig

Alex and Jason share a moment

ANGEL POWER!

separate your paragraphs with blank lines – this makes your posting easier to read.

● If you want to put *emphasis* on certain words, use *asterisks* before and after them instead of using CAPITALS.

● Always be polite. If no one replies to one of your postings, leave it. Never demand reactions to your posts – people will only think you're acting like a spoilt brat.

● Don't include the entire contents of a previous posting in your reply – just enough to remind people what was being talked about and what your take on it is.
> Remember:
> The previous posting is often indented
> with arrows in this way.

Bear these simple rules in mind and you'll avoid upsetting others and getting flamed! And remember, there's nothing cool about trampling over other people's thoughts and feelings, even if you think you know better. For instance, Alex is always careful to leave the love-struck members of Jason's newsgroup with their dreams, no matter how tempting it is to tell them the truth about his smelly feet and bad habits!

SAY IT WITH SYMBOLS

While Natalie loves the excitement of chattering on-line to buddies in cyberspace, she's always aware that people can't see her or hear her when she's saying her stuff. She hates people taking her words the wrong way. If she tells Dylan to her face that she should go to a hair-stylist who isn't blind, then Dylan can see she's only teasing. But if Dylan read it in a note, she might think Natalie was being serious and end up feeling hurt.

Luckily, there's a whole lot of ways to make clear the 'tone of voice' you're using when you talk on the Internet. They're patterns of keyboard characters called emoticons, and here are the ones Natalie uses most. If you don't get them at first sight, try turning the page a quarter-turn clockwise ...

:-) I'm smiling

:-|) I'm laughing

;-) I'm teasing you

:-(I'm sad

:'-(I'm crying

[:-(I'm frowning

I'm shocked or surprised

:-p I'm sticking out my tongue at you

:-L—— I'm drooling at the thought of it

But Natalie's very favourite emoticon, both to send and to receive, is this:

@—'-,——

A single, long-stemmed romantic red rose – electronic style!

WHAT NEXT?

The Internet continues to grow at an incredible rate. It's not going away, and it's clearly going to shape and dominate our futures more and more. Whether everyone on the planet ends up connected to the Net ... whether we'll attend virtual schools and offices, learning and working while never leaving our homes ... or whether we'll one day download books like this and print them out ourselves rather than go and buy them in a shop ... You can help shape that future for yourself. Don't be left off-line and fall behind. Join the Angels in getting to grips with Internet issues *now*!

ANGELIC TO THE MAX!

As you might guess from the Angels' lifestyle and backgrounds, when it comes to sporting pastimes, these girls aren't going to be playing lawn bowls or croquet! They don't let the years pass them by – they live life to the full.

The Angels' sporting talents are vital to their work – they never know when they might be called upon to parachute from a plane, abseil down a tower block or sprint after a bad guy. But there are some sports they love just for the buzz. If you want to take your own Angel Power to similar extremes, maybe you could think about doing some of the following …

GO-CARTING COOL

You're screaming round the track in your ground-hugging racing cart … the world is a blur of speed around you as you focus on the twisting track ahead … You slow down to take the corner, but not enough – you feel your back wheels sliding out, but then rev the engine and accelerate into the skid, getting the cart back under control. With a scream of engines another racer tears past you. Gritting your teeth, you swing wildly round the next corner in hot pursuit …

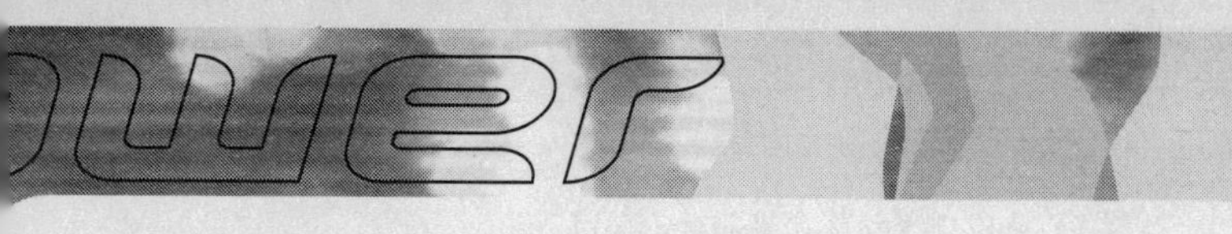

Go-carting is a real thrill – it's certainly car-crazy Natalie's favourite pastime – and you don't need a driving licence to take part! Most tracks will allow under-sixteens to have a go. Check out your local track and make sure it's big on safety – there should be no contact allowed between cars and special signals given in case of danger.

Once that's sorted, it's time for action! There are no complicated gears to worry about, just one pedal to accelerate and one pedal to brake! Large groups are catered for and you can all race against each other – or just enjoy a jaunt round the track at your leisure. The carts can reach speeds of up to thirty miles per hour; it may not sound like much but when you're that close to the ground and taking the hairpin bends it seems a lot faster!

Angel Action Rating: 4 out of 5

HORSE-SENSE

Your horse gallops up to the water jump. Crouched down in the saddle, you hear his hooves thudding into the ground. Then your stomach lurches as your horse rears up and jumps. You're flying through the air for a moment, grinning wildly as you clear the jump. You hear a splash as his back legs just catch the shallow water, then the sound is lost as the crashing applause of the onlookers in the arena fills your ears, and you charge on to the next obstacle ...

Alex won no end of trophies for horse riding in her childhood – but whether you want to enter trials and gymkhanas or just trot on quiet roads, riding a horse is fantastic fun.

There should be a riding school in your area, so go

check it out – and, again, make sure they're big on safety. Talk to some of the students and see if they rate it. If you think you'll get on there, sign up. But don't be surprised if you find you don't spend much time – if any – on a horse in your first lesson. You have to learn how to care for your horse, how not to scare it, how to sit correctly, and how to get back down from it before you can go charging off!

Once you have some experience, you'll be able to ride on your own. If you're really keen, you might like to consider riding in competitions! It takes a lot of time and work to build a good relationship with your horse. But when you feel ready to compete you can try everything from show jumping – where you must clear fences, mud banks and ditches – to competitive trail riding, where horse and owner are judged on covering a specified distance within a time limit. Whatever you choose, and however good you are, if you enjoy yourself and look out for the horse, you'll always be a winner!

Angel Action Rating: 3 out of 5

DIVE DEEPER

Your breath comes out in bubbles through your regulator as you push out with your legs and propel yourself deeper down into the clear indigo water. Through your mask you see shoals of fish flash by … you wonder what they make of you in your pink fins and bright-yellow air tanks. The pressure builds in your ear and you swallow to equalize. It's amazing here under the sea, and breathtakingly beautiful …

Seventy-one per cent of this planet is made up of water – isn't it time you got to exploring some of it yourself? The

Angels are all natural water babies, just as likely to crash into the sea after tumbling from an out-of-control helicopter as they are to dive in from the top board – but basic swimming skills are all you need to start scuba-diving yourself.

If there's a reputable dive centre near you and you're over twelve years old, you can take a course and get certified. But a popular way to try out scuba-diving is by enrolling on a recognized course while on holiday. You'll get used to the equipment, learn safety tips in the pool, then be taken on a guided shallow dive, with your instructor on hand at all times to check you're OK. From there it's up to you if you want to take it further!

If diving seems a bit too intense for you, give snorkelling a go. You stay near the surface of the water and breathe through your snorkel – a long pipe that sticks out of the water and into the air. Without needing to keep coming up for air, you can stare around underwater for as long as you like!

Angel Action Rating: 4 out of 5

'SNOW BIGGER BUZZ!

Gliding over the white carpet of snow on your board, your heart races with excitement as you ride up to the hit. You're cruising at a steady speed, knees bent, fully focused – no edging or skidding at the last moment for you! Your legs are like coiled springs and as you near the top of the jump, you push up into the air. The ground drops away beneath you, your heart rises into your mouth and you're soaring through cold blue sky, free as a bird …

Snowboarding – basically skateboarding crossed with skiing – is fast, furious fun, and more and more people are trying it out on their holidays. Unlike skiing, there are no poles involved – you slide across the snow on a big board.

If you fancy a go, then a good way of seeing if you're up to it – and up *for* it – is to practise boarding on an artificial ski slope. It's worth looking around because, while some of the older slopes are made of stuff called Dendix (it's like you're gliding over toothbrush bristles, which can hurt if you fall off), other more modern slopes actually use real snow, which is more fun and hurts a lot less! There will be equipment available to hire, but don't forget to wear protective clothing, as you should expect a few bumps!

Angel Action Rating: 4 out of 5

JUMP FOR JOY!

You're a long, long way up – and you're going down. Your heart's pounding. The countdown begins: 5 … 4 … You check your safety harness. 3 … 2 … 1 … Go! Time seems to slow as you push off from the bridge. You yell at the top of your lungs as the water far below rushes up to meet you, closer, closer until the cords tug on your harness and you stop, just a couple of metres from the glassy surface of the water. Before you can even breathe a sigh of relief you're catapulted back up into the sky …

Bungee jumping – you can do it from bridges, cranes, towers, even hot-air balloons! It's been a cool craze for some time now, and for sheer thrills and adventure the bungee experience is hard to beat. Look on the Net for safe, reputable companies offering safe and secure bungee jumping – and check to see whether any age limits apply. Remember, though, this sport really is extreme, and you may want to leave it to fully qualified Angels!

Angel Action Rating: 5 out of 5

ANGEL ACTION HEAVEN

The Angels are highly trained and have spent years practising extreme sports. Don't be dismayed if you fancy a go and things don't fall into place straight away. You'll pick up no end of brilliant memories to go with your bumps and bruises as you learn. And never feel pressured into trying to perform amazing stunts. Just keeping fit and enjoying slightly gentler sports can up your Angel Power to the max ... Enjoy!

CHILLING OUT!

When you're as busy and active as the Angels, it's important to know when to drop down a gear and get the most from some quality downtime. But each of the Angels has her own ideas of what to get up to when the case is closed and it's time for some serious relaxation.

ALEX – HOT STUFF

Natalie's surname may be 'Cook', but it's Alex who dreams of being a master chef! But, strange as it sounds, Alex just cannot get the hang of the whole cooking thing. Ask her to strip down the oven into component parts and she'll do it in under an hour – but ask her to bake a cake and you never know *what* you're going to end up with!

Making and baking your own food is good fun. There's certainly nothing 'wifey' about knowing how to cook – in fact, many top chefs are men! But before you try out a recipe make sure you ask permission before you go using someone else's ingredients or dirtying their pans!

Start practising with simple recipes like omelettes, pancakes, stir-fries or croque-monsieur. Timing is key to cookery – so try and have most things you'll need ready before you begin. Keep your head even if your creation is

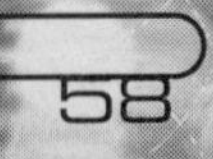

coming apart – how it tastes is the important thing, making it look nice too will come with practice! Most importantly, have a good laugh and don't get put off if it all goes horribly messy and wrong the first few times!

Once you've mastered the basic techniques, you'll find your confidence growing to the point where you can turn your hand to more or less anything! Experiment with different herbs or ingredients, see which foods go best together, learn what works and what doesn't – and suddenly you'll find yourself popular with a lot of very hungry friends!

Here's a recipe for the sweet treat that has foiled Alex time and time again. Bosley and the other Angels nick-name her creations Chinese Fighting Muffins – deadlier than a hand-grenade when hurled at an enemy – but if you make them, hopefully they'll just be good old plain blueberry!

ALEX'S ANGELIC BLUEBERRY MUFFINS

This recipe makes twelve magnificent muffins!
You'll need:
A large mixing bowl
A small mixing bowl
An egg whisk
A wooden spoon
Muffin cases (like cake cases, only bigger)
A baking tray
Oven gloves
A wire tray

Ingredients:

450 g white flour
3 tablespoons castor sugar
Half a teaspoon of salt
1 teaspoon baking powder
1 large free-range egg
40 g butter
225 ml milk
55 ml water
1.5 cups of blueberries

Method:

1. Pre-heat the oven to 180° C/350° F/Gas Mark 4 (make sure you ask an adult first – they may want to do some cooking themselves!)

2. Sift the flour, the sugar, the salt and the baking powder together in the large mixing bowl. Make a well in the centre.

3. Put the egg, the butter, the milk and the water into the small mixing bowl and whisk them together until no lumps remain.

4. Pour the egg mixture into the well in the large bowl and use the wooden spoon to gently stir it all in. Add the blueberries a few at a time until they are mixed well in.

5. Spoon the mixture into the muffin cups until each is two-thirds full. Put them on a baking tray and, wearing oven gloves, place them in the oven and bake for thirty to thirty-five minutes.

6. Carefully take the risen muffins out of the oven (don't forget the oven gloves!) and leave them to cool on the wire tray for five to ten minutes.

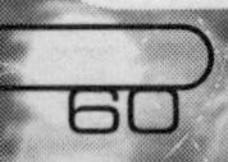

7. Ask some special friends round and see what they make of your creations. Stuff your face! And if the muffins aren't completely Angelic the first time … just try again!

NATALIE – LEARNING THE LANGUAGE

When Natalie's body is worn out fighting crime, her mind's still wide awake – so her way of kicking back is sticking her gorgeous head deep in a book. But while she enjoys a good novel as much as the rest of us, her real love is learning new languages.

Chances are you're already learning a language in school right now – probably French or German. As the countries in Europe grow closer together, knowing another European language is becoming more and more useful. And as the Internet continues to pull the whole *world* closer together, being able to communicate in other languages has never been more important.

It's true that lots of people in the world speak English and that you could get by without learning another language, but that attitude is small-minded, lazy and definitely lacking in Angel Power!

Try out some of Natalie's favourite phrases – the way to say the foreign words is written beneath them, to help you get your tongue in gear!

1. I'm a super secret agent!

In German:
Ich bin eine super Agentin!
ick binn eye-ner super ah-gent-in

In French:
Je suis agent 'top-secret' formidable!
je sweez ah-jon 'top secret' for-mee-dah-bl

In Spanish:
Soy agente super-secreta!
soy a-hent-ay super sek-ret-a

2. Coming through!

In German:
Wir kommen!
veer komm-men

In French:
Laissez-moi passer!
leh-sey mwa pass-eh

In Spanish:
Cuidado, ya voy!
cwee-dad-o ya voy

3. Girls are good, but Angels are better!

In German:
Madchen sind gut, aber Engeln sind besser!
mayd-chin sint goot arber eng-uln sint bess-er

In French:
Les filles sont magnifiques, les Anges sont encore mieux!
Leh fee son man-yee-feek, lez onge sont ahng-cor mee-yer

In Spanish:
Las chicas son majas, los Angeles son aun mejor
lass cheek-as son ma-has, loss an-hell-ess sonn a-oon may-hor

4. I love you!

In German:
Ich liebe dich!
Ick leeber dick

In French:
Je t'aime!
Je tairm

In Spanish:
Te quiero!
Ter kee-air-o

The words may sound strange on your tongue, but with practice you'll soon be speaking them like a local. Want to find out more? Then get down to your local library or local high-street bookshop where you'll find a lot of language courses on CD or cassette. Or go on-line and check out what language classes are running in your area.

DYLAN – PLAYING POOL

When Dylan needs to unwind she likes to hang out and shoot some pool with her friends. She finds it far more satisfying to break at pool than to break some thug's head!

You'll find pool tables in lots of places like youth centres, amusement arcades and snooker clubs. Pool is a game of skill for two or four players, and it's also known as bar billiards or 8-ball. The rules are fairly simple – but the game is a lot harder than it looks!

Basically, there are a white cue ball and fifteen coloured balls on the pool table. Each player uses a long wooden cue to knock the cue ball (white ball) against one of the coloured balls, aiming to knock it (or 'sink' it) into a pocket. One player must pocket the balls that are solid colours (or else just the yellow balls), while the other player must pocket the balls that are striped (or else just the red balls). The player who pockets his group first must then pocket the black ball, or 8-ball, to win the game.

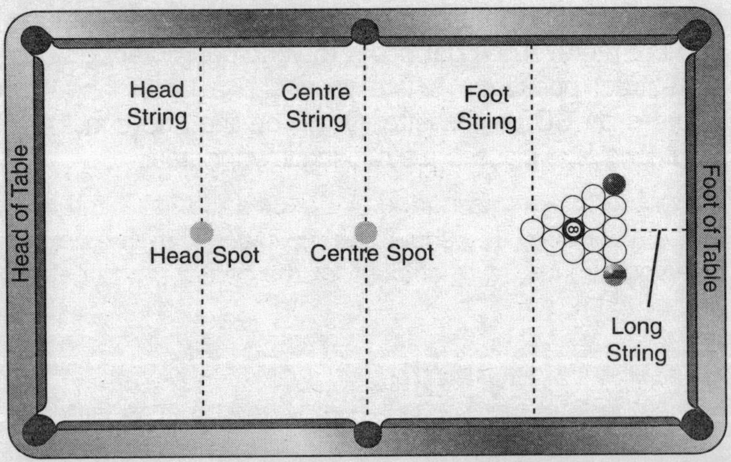

Dylan has a few tips for beginners wanting to give this great game a try!

1. Choose hands

Here's how you can tell which hand you'll use to hold your cue and which you'll rest it on – your 'lean hand'. Point the index finger of your right hand out in front of you and close your left eye. If you're still pointing straight ahead, you should hold the cue in your right hand and lean on your left. If it's pointing to the left, you need to hold the cue in your left hand and lean on your right.

2. Lean in

Your body position should be comfortable and steady when taking a shot, so start by standing in front of the table with your feet about the same distance apart as your shoulders. Move your lean foot (the same as your lean hand!) one step towards the table. Then bend your body forward. Rest your cue on your lean hand between thumb and forefinger and look ahead straight over the cue to line up the shot.

3. Cue ball

If you're breaking – that is, if you're beginning the game by hitting the balls for the first time with the cue ball – you need to put a lot of ANGEL POWER into that first strike. So put your lean hand about ten centimetres away from the cue ball and practise moving the cue back and forth – the only part of your body that should be moving is your cue arm to give you strength. Aim straight for the centre of the ball ... and hit it there!

4. All in the angle

Remember, the ball you're aiming for will move differently

depending on where you hit it. If you hit the ball dead in the centre, it will move straight ahead. If the impact is more to the right of the ball, the ball will move more to the left, and it works the same the other way round. Who'd have thought maths could be so cool!

SET YOUR OWN PACE

That's three very different ways of relaxing for three very different Angels. So the next time you're slobbing in front of the TV, remember that you *do* have other options. You can take a hobby easy or go mad over it, but whatever speed you want to take things, just feel happy knowing you're maximizing your spare time – and working up your Angel Power too!

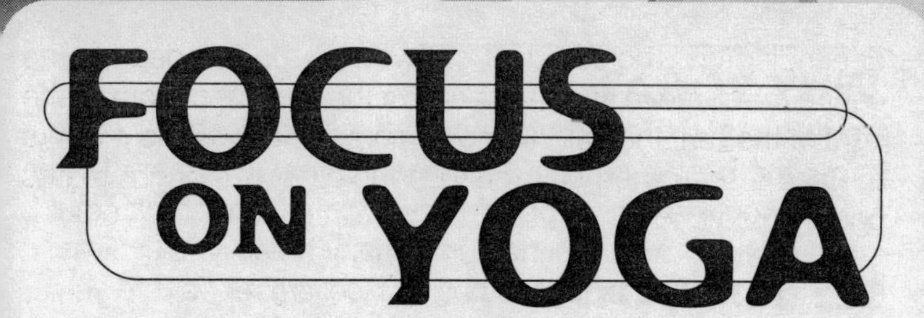

When Dylan was growing up she was quite a wild child, but eventually she realized she was on a path that was doing her harm. That's one of the reasons she started practising yoga – a great way to exercise your mind, body and spirit!

It may be very fashionable at the moment, but yoga is much more than just a fad – it's been around for thousands of years! There are bound to be classes being held in your area NOW. If not, you can teach yourself at home from a book or a video. Every girl can use yoga as a means of getting in touch with her own special Angel Power!

WHY YOGA?

Yoga is not just an exercise but a whole philosophy of life – but the best thing is, it can mean as much or as little to you as you like. Some people see yoga as a good workout once a week, others bring it into many areas of their lives. You can take and enjoy the bits you feel are relevant to you, and leave the rest. Here's the lowdown to help you decide:

1. Yoga's a fantastic physical exercise programme
It teaches you how to stretch, makes you more flexible and strengthens your spine and all your joints.

2. Yoga teaches breathing techniques and relaxation
You'll feel calmer and more relaxed – important at stressful times like exams or sports trials – and so better able to enjoy your action-packed life!

3. Yoga teaches meditation
Meditation doesn't have to mean sitting with others in a circle and chanting funny words. It's a great way of increasing your concentration and calming your mind if you're upset.

4. Yoga teaches a whole philosophy
It can help you become aware of your mind and body, and teaches you to question everything until you find the answer yourself and understand it.

CHOOSING A PATH

There are many different types of yoga ...

Hatha Yoga

This can be translated from the Sanskrit as 'sun and moon yoga'. In the Hatha style of yoga, the emphasis is placed on getting the most out of different positions and postures, while focusing on your breathing. You rest between getting into each position, so it's perhaps the easiest style of yoga to do, increasing health and fitness and using the body as a way of connecting with the mind.

Mantra Yoga

This is the yoga of sound – a mantra is made up of words or syllables repeated over and over again until the meaning is absorbed into the mind to bring great concentration and inner peace.

Ashtanga Yoga

Ashtanga can be translated from the Sanskrit as 'The eight-limbed path'. It's also known as 'Power yoga' and is very popular in America, made famous by Ashtanga students such as Madonna! Unlike Hatha yoga, in Ashtanga you don't pause for breath – you just move straight from one position to the next. People who do Ashtanga yoga regularly get fitter and stronger and noticeably more muscular.

SOUL GUIDE

Regardless of which type of yoga you choose, there are ten common-sense yogic guidelines that all students should follow. These are *yammas* (the way we deal with the outside world) and *niyamas* (the way we treat ourselves). They're not about being right or wrong, just about being honest with yourself. Here, Dylan's put a twist on these guidelines to make them every Angel's code of honour!

Ahisma: Kindness

Be gentle in action, thought and speech at all times.
ANGEL TWIST: Not always easy when you're up against some of the biggest bruisers around, but the Angels only fight back when there's no other option.

Satya: Truthfulness

Know when to be honest.
ANGEL TWIST: That doesn't necessarily mean you have to tell your mate that her new party outfit makes her look like a Christmas-tree fairy!

Asteya: Non-stealing

Don't be jealous of what you don't have.
ANGEL TWIST: Use your natural abilities to get what you want honestly, no matter how long it takes.

Brahmacharya: Moderation

Don't over-indulge in the things you enjoy.
ANGEL TWIST: But if you do accidentally demolish a whole tub of ice cream from time to time, don't beat yourself up over it too much – holding on to the experience will only make you feel worse.

Aparigraha: Simplicity

Get for yourself what you really need, not what you think you want.

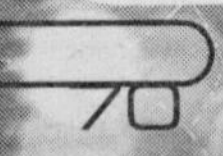

ANGEL TWIST: That's not to say you shouldn't own a really hot pair of trainers – just that you probably don't really need twelve pairs.

Shaucha: Purity

Be good to yourself and keep in good health.
ANGEL TWIST: Roughing up bad guys is an exercise best left to fully qualified Angels only!

Santosha: Contentment

Make the best of things.
ANGEL TWIST: Accept what you can't change, and change what you can – knowing the difference is real Angel Power!

Tapas: Strict discipline

Do regularly what you need to reach your goals.
ANGEL TWIST: See something through, whatever it takes. When you get there, you'll know it's been worth it – and you can eat ice cream to celebrate!

Swadhyaya: Self-education

Wisdom comes from questioning the truth – never accept anything at face value.
ANGEL TWIST: Unless it's been told to you by Charlie!

Ishwara-Pranidhana: Find the spirit

Express your spiritual side by doing the things that stir your soul.
ANGEL TWIST: It might be walking your dog or listening to music or writing poetry – or it might just be saving the world on a daily basis.

SALUTE THE SUN

Dylan's favourite yoga exercise is the 'sun salutation'. Follow this guide and copy the positions. You may feel at first like you're playing some crazy game of Twister, but you'll soon get the hang of it – and start feeling the benefits!

ANGEL TIP: If you find your body can't quite get into all the positions, just try as best you can. The important thing is to breathe in all the right places, and try to make the movements continuous.

1. Stand with both feet touching, facing the sun if it's up! Bring your hands together in front of your chest, as if you're praying.

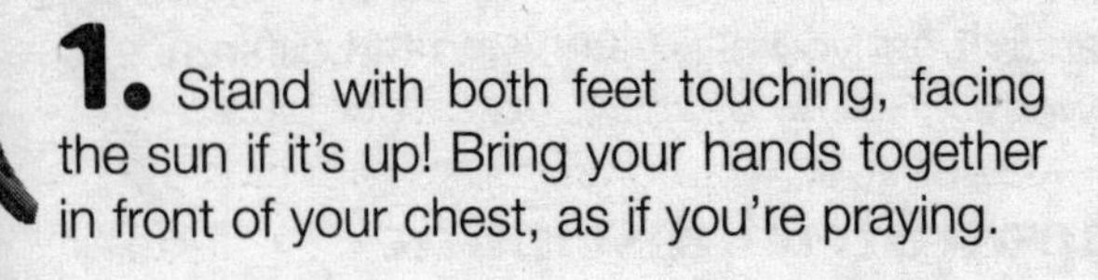

2. Breathe in and raise your arms upwards. Slowly bend backwards with your arms above your head.

3. Breathe out and bend forwards, touching the ground respectfully so that your hands are in line with your feet and your head is touching your knees.

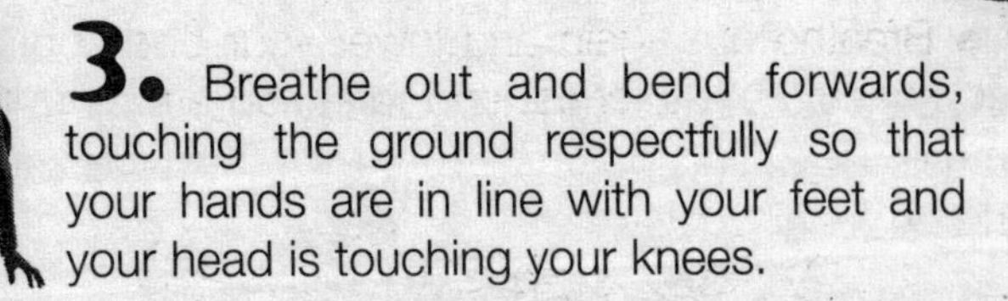

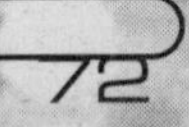

4. Breathe in slowly and move your right leg back away from your body at full stretch. Keep your hands and feet on the ground – your hands should be either side of your left foot – and raise your head.

5. While slowly breathing out, bring your left foot back to join the right foot. Keep your arms straight, raise your hips and lower your head until you're forming an arch.

6. Breathe in and slowly lower your hips until they're just above the ground, holding your weight on your arms and feet. Bend backwards as far as you can.

7. Breathe out again and lower your body until your feet, knees, hands, chest and forehead are all touching the ground.

8. Breathe in, slowly raise your head, and bend backwards as far as possible, while supporting yourself on your hands.

9. Breathe out, keep your arms straight and raise your hips, pushing your bottom in the air until you form an arch.

10. Breathe in, bend your left leg at the knee and bring it forward, placing your left foot firmly on the ground between your hands. Raise your head upwards.

11. Breathe out, keep your hands where they are and bring your right foot forwards to join your left foot between your hands. Lower your head to your knees.

12. Breathe in and raise your arms upwards. Then slowly bend backwards with your arms above your head.

13. Return to your first position, palms pressed together in front of your chest. You've just given your own Angelic salutation to the sun!

PRACTICE MAKES PERFECT

You're probably aching already just from trying those first moves. Perhaps you're wondering if yoga is right for you? Remember the principle of Swadhyaya, and do what any self-respecting Angel would do. Ask some questions, keep an open mind and see how things go.

The most important thing is to make sure you find a certified yoga instructor who can guide you into those body-twisting yoga positions safely. And if you're teaching yourself at home, follow the instructions carefully and never force positions if your body doesn't want to know!

Yoga instructors reckon that practising once a week will gradually loosen you up, practising twice a week will get you in pretty good shape and practising three to five times a week will transform your body and soul and change your life! But one thing's for sure – where yoga's concerned, the truth of the matter is always inside you ... and it's sparkling with 100 per cent Angel Power!

ROOMS FOR IMPROVEMENT

Tired of waking up in the morning and staring around at the same old walls? Perhaps the time has come to put a little of your angelic energies into sassying up your surroundings, Angel-style!

MAKEOVER TIME

Each of Charlie's Angels has a very different and distinct image of her own. Alex is cool, smart and sophisticated. Natalie is soft and feminine, and just that little bit goofy. Dylan is a free spirit, wild but sensitive.

You probably see a bit of yourself in each of them. So why not try taking ideas from their swish Californian residences and use them to transform your room into a place fit for Angels!

DYLAN DECOR

Dylan's pad could be described politely as 'bohemian' – or less so as 'offbeat' or 'a cluttered mess'! It's very distinctly her though, and speaks volumes about the laid-back way she lives her life – always for the moment, making the most of what life puts her way.

If you want the bohemian look yourself, the key is to fill your room with a riot of rich, deep colour, delicious smells and cool and funky objects. Try trawling through car boot sales or charity shops for interesting bric-a-brac to line your shelves with. Cover your walls in quirky prints and paintings – placed around your wall in mismatched frames they'll look kooky cool. And if your flowery bedspread just doesn't cut it any more, buy a piece of funky printed material to throw across your bed, or to make cool cushions for extra splashes of colour.

Dylan also likes burning incense when she's practising her yoga to help her relax. You can find incense burners or scented candles in lots of high-street shops, with different aromas for different moods. However, remember that you must never leave a lighted candle or incense stick unattended.

Lighting should be soft to keep you nice and relaxed, so maybe you could buy a new lampshade. Dylan has a funky lava lamp – these can be a bit expensive, but if your birthday or Christmas is coming up, perhaps you could put one on your wish list. You'll find yourself staring at the shifting shapes and colours for hours!

Finally, why not trawl through some toy shops for a particularly important piece of bric-a-brac for your room: a model car, a '69 Camaro in orange and white? That's what Dylan drives – so you'd be giving just a cool little nod of acknowledgement and respect to your style guru!

ALEX AREA

If there's one word that sums up Alex, it's *impeccable*. She's the kind of girl who never has a hair out of place – and her loft conversion in downtown Los Angeles is much the same. Combining minimalist chic

with feng shui, Alex has created a stylish place to relax ...

If you fancy taking a leaf from Alex's mint-condition book, then you'll need to set aside time every week to make your room seriously tidy. Clear every surface of things you don't really need. But don't just stick stuff anywhere it'll go – out of sight may be out of mind, but you'll be going out of *your* mind looking for things! Sort out all your drawers and cupboards, throw away what you don't need, then pick a place to keep everything else – and make sure it stays there!

Alex likes plain, simple, sophisticated things. Even if you have patterned curtains and teddy-bear wallpaper there are still things you can change. Get a plain neutral-coloured throw and cushions for your bed. And always make sure the bedclothes are ironed and the bed is well made.

Remember, less is more in an Alex area. If your room is cluttered with posters, take most of them down and put up only those that you feel really say something about you. If you can't decide, take them all down and find something new! Perhaps you could go looking for a large mirror in a second-hand shop to put on your wall. This will reflect light and so help your room seem more spacious and bright.

You might find room in your tidy, spotless new habitat for one special ornament: a tiny model silver Mercedes convertible, just like the one Alex drives for real. Who knows, one day, perhaps you'll own one too!

COOK'S QUARTERS

natalie

Since Natalie is a wide-eyed, innocent and go-getting kind of girl, her room is styled in an equally upbeat, easygoing kind of way. Her flat is a total bachelorette pad – she makes no secret of the things she loves and friends can take her just as she comes. Her place is just the way *she* wants it.

It's all about personal taste with Natalie, so think about your interests and the things you like to have around, and how best you can show them off. Design your room around your own needs. What do you collect? You may not have a collection of troll dolls like Natalie does, but whatever you collect, whether it's cuddly toys or posters of your favourite band, make sure you display them proudly. The most important things in Natalie's life are her friends and family – try decorating your walls with framed pictures of your best mates, your pets or your favourite holiday snaps.

Natalie is fanatically tidy. Her CD and record collection is in alphabetical order so she can find what she wants in a matter of moments. Try doing this with your books and videos. Sure, it might seem a little nerdish, but, as Natalie knows, it certainly saves time not having to look for things. Time you can then spend having fun with your mates!

While Natalie may always look trendy, being fashionable is just not something that really concerns her. She knows what she likes and sticks with it – regardless of what the latest trend is. However, there's one cool item you might want to give pride of place in your room – a model of a fly-red Ferrari Modena like the one Natalie drives – some things will *never* go out of fashion!

IT'S YOUR SPACE

Whatever you choose to do with your room, always remember to celebrate your space. Every Angel needs a heavenly place all of her own – so have fun experimenting with different looks until you find the one that's exactly right for YOU!

ANGELIC GYMNASTICS

To help them have the energy, suppleness and strength to perform their mind-blowing, death-defying stunts, the Angels have to really stay in shape. A great way to become as graceful and lithe as any of Charlie's Angels is to take up gymnastics. Dylan, Alex and Natalie have all been doing gym since they were kids – and they have the sleek figures and incredible muscle tone to prove it! You may already do gymnastics at school, or perhaps there's an after-school club or class you could join. Check it out.

ANGEL TIPS FOR TRAINING

1. WARM-UP

Before you go charging into action yourself, take the time to do a good warm-up first with some jogging, skipping, hopping or jumping. It's important to prepare your body for any exercise by increasing your breathing and your heart-rate. Wear warm clothes too – increasing your body heat makes it less likely you'll pull a muscle when stretching.

2. STRETCHING

It's important that you stretch your muscles, ligaments and tendons. To keep your body flexible, you should make sure each part of the body is properly stretched every thirty-six hours. Ask your PE teacher (or a trainer at your local gym if you're a member) for some useful stretching exercises. Find some you can do with a friend, so you can stretch out together!

3. STRENGTH TRAINING

When you're trying to condition your body, it's important to spend time increasing your muscle strength by both lifting weights and working your body through press-ups, sit-ups and squat thrusts. Don't worry about buying weights – you can use textbooks or tins of food. And don't get too carried away – you don't want to strain yourself. Again, ask your PE teacher for advice.

GYM KITTENS

The Angels always incorporate basic gymnastic moves into their fighting styles – and often with a twist ... You'll find a few of these below, along with some top Angel tips to help you on your way!

DANCE Gymnastics and dance are closely linked, and a gymnastic routine is choreographed to make it look as graceful as possible. Top gymnasts have benefited from years of dance training too.

ANGEL TWIST: Dylan's own dance style is pretty out there – after a breathtaking display of gymnastic high-kicks to knock out some bad guys, she likes to *moonwalk* away from the scene of the action!

HANDSTANDS Handstands are a very important skill in gymnastics, used on every piece of apparatus. Try one now, taking your weight on both hands with your palms

flat. Don't worry if you're wobbly at first. Try performing the handstand in front of a wall so you can balance against it. Then find the point of balance with your hands and take your heels away from the wall. How long can you stay upright unaided?

ANGEL TWIST: Wear leggings or a leotard when doing handstands for comfort.

CARTWHEELING If your cartwheels aren't straight, get hold of some crash mats and place them up against the wall. Try a cartwheel right in front of them, facing the wall – now your legs can't fall forwards!

ANGEL TIP: Keep control of your body by spending equal time on foot, hand, hand and foot as you cartwheel.

VAULTING Never mind the complicated moves you need to make when you're working your body over the vault – what about getting on to it in the first place? The key to success in vaulting is a good fast run-up, lifting your knees high and with strong arm action.

ANGEL TWIST: Angels often need a good run-up at lots of things, whether it's to go grappling with the Thin Man when he's scaling a wall (like Alex) or to leap across a criss-cross laser security system in the heart of Red Star International's programming hub (like Natalie) ...

BEAM The secret of staying on the beam is to keep your hips and shoulders square to the beam and parallel with each other, so that your centre of gravity is steady over the beam at all times. You can turn out your feet slightly and grip the sides of the beam with your toes for extra balance. Practise at first with just a line drawn on the floor. Then you can progress to a floor beam, and finally to the high beam itself – just leave plenty of mats underneath for a while!

ANGEL TIP: A good trick is to keep your head up, so you don't look at what your feet are doing. Instead, look down your nose at the end of the beam to help keep you in line.

GET THE RHYTHM

Even if you decide the beam is bad news and you can't cope with the vault, don't give up on gymnastics just yet … there are other types you can try.

Almost forty years ago, the International Gymnastics Federation recognized rhythmic gymnastics as a sport, and there have been world championships ever since.

Your physical training won't have been wasted, as each movement of a rhythmic gymnastics routine is highly athletic. You'll need strength, power, agility, flexibility and endurance – all the classic Angel attributes!

Rhythmic gymnastics means you have to exercise your body using different pieces of apparatus – and all to music! If your school doesn't support this kind of gymnastics, have a look around your local area for a club or gym that does. There are five basic props you will find yourself using if you decide to have a go.

ROPE You can choose what colour your rope is, and whether you want to hold it in one hand or two. Its length is in proportion to your height. The best rhythmic gymnasts can make the rope seem like a shimmering snake whipping and coiling and whirling round them as they effortlessly and elegantly dance – a truly explosive effect!

HOOP Either wood or plastic, the hoop is used to define a space inside which the rhythmic gymnast moves.

Frequent changes of grip are required, as the gymnast rolls through it, jumps in and out of it, high-tosses it, and so on, never missing the beat and rhythm of the music.

BALL Weighing at least 400 grams, the rubber or plastic ball must not be gripped, only caught lightly and returned to the air. The ball must move in perfect harmony with the gymnast, who uses split-second timing, throwing, rolling and balancing it with breathtaking control and precision.

CLUBS Particularly suited to ambidextrous gymnasts (those who can use both hands equally well), the wooden or plastic clubs – each one around half a metre long – are used to execute throws, rolls and twists and to describe incredible shapes in the air. Gymnasts using the clubs need an impeccable sense of rhythm and extraordinary timing.

RIBBON The ribbon, which must be at least six metres long, may be thrown in different directions to create designs and shapes in the air. Snakes, spirals and throws must all be carried out expertly to different rhythms as the gymnast dances, and the ribbon must remain in constant motion!

ROUNDING OFF

Whichever style of gymnastics you try, whether it's graceful or powerful, give it everything you can and your Angel Power is sure to grow. Dylan, Alex and Natalie are all top-class gymnasts – see if you can follow in their feather-light footsteps!

SO WHAT MAKES AN ANGEL?

If you've read this far, then you've got to know each of Charlie's Angels and the fast-paced world they live in. But what of the Angels of the future?

Imagine you're in Charlie's office ... Bosley's sitting behind the desk chipping in, while Charlie's conducting your job interview long-range over a hidden transmitter. Reckon you've got what it takes to be one of the Angels? Let the quiz decide ... Answer the questions, then tot up your score and see if you make the grade.

1. Charlie asks you why you're applying for the job of Angel-for-hire. Do you say ...?

a) I hear the money and benefits are great.
b) I want to fight crime as part of the best team around.
c) Crime's the disease and I'm the cure.

2. Bosley leans forward and asks you, 'Parlez-vous français?' Do you reply ...?

a) Yes, a little.
b) Mais oui! Bien sûr!
c) Sorry, I don't speak German.

3. Charlie asks you how you feel about fighting bad guys. Do you say ...?

a) I'll only fight if there's no other way.

b) If they've done something wrong, I'll sure teach them not to do it again.

c) I'll only fight if you insure my perfect nails against breaking.

4. Bosley wonders if you hold a black belt. Do you reply ...?

a) Yes, but it doesn't match these shoes so I left it at home.

b) Yes, in Tae-Kwon-Do.

c) Actually, I'm a professor of Ju-jitsu.

5. Bosley goes on to ask what 'Karate' means. Do you answer ...?

a) A martial art.

b) Empty fist.

c) Empty head.

6. Charlie asks if you'd be prepared to fly to any possible trouble spot in the world for weeks at a time with no warning. Do you answer ...?

a) I'll do whatever I have to.

b) Sure – if nothing else it's a free trip abroad, right.

c) Could be a good opportunity to try out my language skills.

7. Bosley asks if you think you could keep your missions secret from anyone who might want to know. Do you reply ...?

a) Do I have official clearance to answer that question?

b) Could I at least tell my mother?

c) I wouldn't tell a soul.

8. Charlie asks if you're a good team player. Do you reply ...?

a) Yes, I'd try to use my strengths to the team's advantage.

b) Depends if the others take me for granted or not

c) Sure – as long as I'm the leader.

9. Bosley wants to know how you'd set about finding someone who's on the run. Do you answer ...?

a) I'd post requests for information on the Internet.

b) I'd check out where they were seen last and ask witnesses for information.

c) I'd ask their friends if there was a place the missing person would go to when in trouble, and take it from there.

10. Charlie asks how soon you'd be able to start. Do you reply ...?

a) I'd like to meet the other Angels before I decide, just to see how we hang together.

b) Whenever.

c) I'd need to tie up some loose ends from my old life first – but I'm worth the wait.

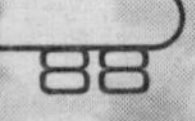

ANSWERS

1. a) 0 b) 4 c) 2
2. a) 2 b) 4 c) 0
3. a) 4 b) 1 c) 0
4. a) 0 b) 3 c) 4
5. a) 1 b) 4 c) 0
6. a) 3 b) 1 c) 4
7. a) 4 b) 0 c) 2
8. a) 4 b) 0 c) 0
9. a) 1 b) 3 c) 4
10. a) 2 b) 2 c) 4

HOW DID YOU SCORE?

30–40 points

Congratulations – you keep a cool head under pressure, you're confident and collected, and your answers are thoughtful and intelligent. You respect yourself and expect others to do the same – you'll be a fantastic Angel-for-hire!

15–29 points

Perhaps you should think a little more carefully before opening your mouth. It's not that you haven't got a lot to say, just that sometimes you let rip at the wrong moment. But the important thing is that you've got bags of potential to better yourself and succeed in the future.

4–14 points

Oh dear! Unfortunately, you're not quite as smart as you'd like to think you are! At the moment you want to be an Angel for all the wrong reasons. Take the time to work out what it is you really want to do in life. Have faith in yourself, and with patience and determination you'll be able to develop your latent Angel Power in the future!

CONCLUSION

CA3 = ACTION!

The only thing that seems to stay the same in today's world is that everything must change. Life has never moved faster, and there's never been a better time to jump aboard and enjoy the ride into who-knows-where.

Whatever the Angels have to face, they will go on having the best times and the wildest adventures. Life for them is quite a party. And it can be for you too. Somewhere out there are adventures, new experiences and like-minded people – all waiting for *you* to have the most awesome time you can imagine.

Whether you live life to the full and make your dreams happen is up to you. Take your lead from the Angels and make sure that your life story winds up filed under A for Action … and stamped top secret with an extra A – for

Angel Power!

ANGEL POWER CHECKLIST

Now you've been shown the way to capitalize on your own unique Angel Power, why not copy out the form on the next page. It's Charlie's checklist for all aspiring Angels. For the professional touch, try typing it up on a PC and making it look really funky! Use it as a record of your life at this moment – and how it could be in the future.

Remember, fill in the form *honestly* – and if you say you're going to do something, make sure you turn the dream into reality. That's what being a true Angel is all about!

My name is..

Height:..

Eyes: ....

Hair: ....

I am most like ....from *Charlie's Angels*

My current hobbies are ....

My best friend and Angel Power Partner is.............................

I am going to find out more about:

- ❏ Martial arts
- ❏ Go-Carting
- ❏ Horse riding
- ❏ Pool
- ❏ Scuba-diving
- ❏ Yoga
- ❏ Snowboarding
- ❏ Gymnastics
- ❏ Skateboarding
- ❏ The Internet

I am planning to join a club to start learning..........................

I will cook..........delicious things every week

I can speak English/French/German/Spanish/Other

....

I am going to learn to speak ....

I promise to act like a true Angel at all times and be worthy of my Angel Power.

Signed: ....

Countersigned ...Charles Townsend...

CHARL

ANGE

ANGEL

CHA

ANG

POWER

RLIE'S

ELS